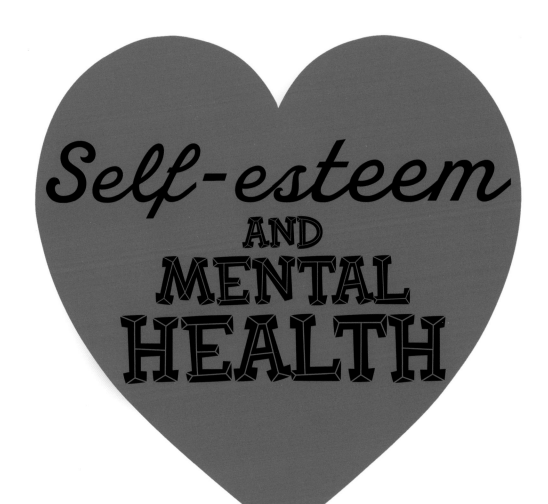

HEALTHY FOR LIFE

Self-esteem AND MENTAL HEALTH

Anna Claybourne

W

FRANKLIN WATTS
LONDON • SYDNEY

Franklin Watts
First published in Great Britain in 2016 by The Watts Publishing Group

Copyright © The Watts Publishing Group, 2016

Credits
Series editors: Sarah Peutrill and Sarah Ridley
Series design and illustrations: Dan Bramall
Cover designers: Peter Scoulding and Cathryn Gilbert

Additional pictures by Shutterstock.com

ISBN 978 1 4451 4979 0

Printed in China

Franklin Watts
An imprint of
Hachette Children's Group
Part of The Watts Publishing Group
Carmelite House
50 Victoria Embankment
London EC4Y 0DZ
An Hachette UK Company
www.hachette.co.uk

www.franklinwatts.co.uk

CONTENTS

The mind and the self

Whenever you're awake, your mind is busy thinking, understanding and reacting. You have thoughts, feelings, ideas, opinions, beliefs, memories, likes and dislikes. These things give you a sense of who you are – your 'self'.

All in your head?

For most people, the mind and the self feel as if they are somewhere inside your head, just behind your eyes. That's because that's where your brain is – the part of your body where thoughts, emotions and ideas happen.

However, the brain also controls the rest of the body, and your emotions can affect your body too. For example, feeling scared can make your heart pound, make you feel sick, or give you 'butterflies in your stomach'.

Mental health

The word 'mental' means to do with the mind, and 'mental health' means the health of your mind, emotions and sense of self.

As you know, your body can fall ill. If you catch a bad cold you may feel shivery, tired and horrible. You have to take a day off school or cancel an arrangement so that you can get better.

In the same way, your mind and emotions can get 'ill' – and this is known as mental illness. It can be caused by stress, pressure or something bad happening in your life. It's often caused by a combination of stressful things getting on top of you.

> I hate this school.

> There are also medicines that can help with some mental illnesses.

Like physical illnesses, there are things you can do to help you feel better – such as talking to someone about your problems, finding ways to relax, or doing a hobby to take your mind off things.

Self-esteem

Self-esteem means how you feel about yourself. If you have healthy (or high) self-esteem you like yourself, and feel confident about who you are. You are happy to have a go at things, and don't get too downhearted when things go wrong.

> Healthy self-esteem doesn't mean you're big-headed. It just means you're happy in your own skin, and accept yourself.

Low self-esteem means not liking or accepting yourself much. You may feel that you're a bad person, that you're useless or worthless, or that you can't get anything right.

Self-esteem is closely linked to mental illness. Low self-esteem makes it harder to cope with bad feelings, difficult situations and stress. It can make people feel angry, confused or despairing.

Staying healthy

It is as important to look after your mental health as your physical health. There are lots of ways to do this that will help you stay as well as possible. You'll find out more about them in this book.

The brain

Your brain is your body's HQ. It takes in information from your senses and controls your movements. It thinks, understands, plans, imagines and remembers. It's where 'you' – your mind, your ideas and emotions, and your personality – can be found.

Superbrain

The brain is INCREDIBLY complicated. It may look like a blob of wrinkly greyish-pink jelly, but inside it's actually more like the world's cleverest computer.

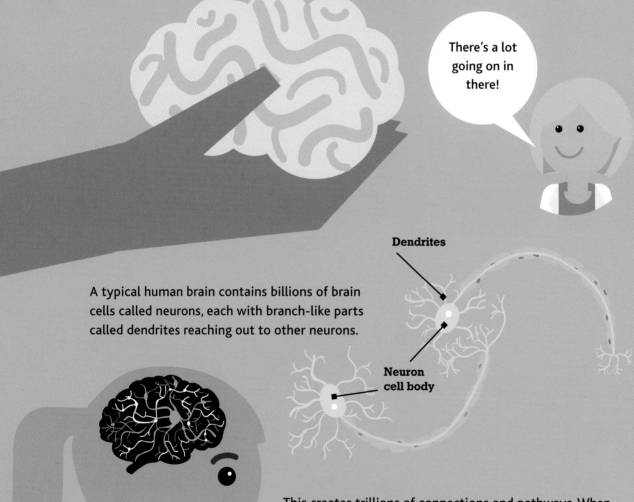

There's a lot going on in there!

A typical human brain contains billions of brain cells called neurons, each with branch-like parts called dendrites reaching out to other neurons.

Dendrites

Neuron cell body

This creates trillions of connections and pathways. When you think, chemical and electrical signals are zooming around your brain, jumping from one neuron to another.

Plastic brain

What's more, the brain is 'plastic'! That doesn't mean it's made of plastic, like a water bottle or a carrier bag. Instead, it means that your brain can change. Whenever you have a new experience or learn something, your brain forms new connections and pathways. The more times you repeat the learning experience, by working out a particular type of maths problem, or practising a musical instrument for instance, the stronger the connection becomes.

This means that your experiences have a big effect on who you are. They literally 'shape' your brain, and the way it works inside. This is one of the reasons we are all so different, and have different personalities.

The teenage brain

When you're growing up, and especially when you're a teenager, your brain is changing very quickly.

From about the age of 13, the brain begins to get rid of some old connections it no longer needs, while making others stronger.

Frontal lobe

Some parts of the brain grow faster than others. For example, the limbic system, which controls strong emotions such as fear and anger, develops faster than some parts of the frontal lobe, which control sensible decision-making.

The brain also releases body chemicals called hormones, to help your body change as you grow up. This includes things like boys' voices getting deeper, and girls having periods.

All these things can make being a teenager extra-stressful.

Emotions can feel so strong, they're overwhelming.

Moods can change fast, so you feel like you're on an emotional rollercoaster.

Your brain is fully developed by about the age of 25, but continues to change throughout your life.

Teenagers are sometimes influenced by others to do things they might regret.

Self-esteem

Esteem means what you think of people, and self-esteem means what you think of yourself – whether that's good or bad. It has a big effect on your mental health.

My feelings matter.

I know what I want, and what I don't want.

I know I'll be useless at that, so I won't try.

No one likes me.

I'll try new things – even if I get them wrong at first.

I'm no good at anything.

I'll never succeed at anything.

I'll stand up for what I believe in.

If I feel sad or hurt, I know it will get better in time.

My feelings don't matter.

They won't want to be my friend.

I like being me.

I don't deserve to be treated well.

I hate myself...

I deserve kindness and respect.

I accept myself, including my failings.

High self-esteem

Low self-esteem

Of course, most of us don't fit into either of these two extremes. People are usually a bit of a mixture. Your self-esteem can go up and down, depending on what's going on in your life.

What causes low self-esteem?

Lots of things can cause people to develop low self-esteem. They can include:

• Being treated badly, especially as a child
• Being bullied or left out at school
• Suffering an attack or abuse
• An upsetting event, such as parents splitting up
• Finding schoolwork difficult or impossible, which can make you feel like a failure.

Low self-esteem problems

It can sometimes be hard for people to realise they have low self-esteem.
Feeling like this is not very nice, so people might not admit it, even to themselves.

This can lead to people showing a range of behaviour including:

- Not completing homework out of fear that it will not be good enough

- Boasting or showing off to hide their true feelings or achievements

- Being very timid and not joining in or making friends

- Experimenting with smoking, drugs or alcohol, to impress others or distract from their true feelings.

Low-self esteem can also contribute to mental illness, because it can make people feel very sad, stressed, worthless or out of control. Some people hear a voice in their head saying negative things, which can be really alarming. Low self-esteem is linked to things like:

- Underachievement, when people stop studying or trying to learn

- Self-harm, when people injure themselves on purpose (see page 15)

- Eating disorders, which affect the way people eat (see page 19)

- Depression, a mental illness that can make people feel sad or numb (see page 14).

Look after your self-esteem

Here are a few ideas for how to improve your self-esteem:

- Set yourself small goals or challenges, and try hard to achieve them – it will feel good.
- Spend time doing things you enjoy.
- Do something creative, like drawing, cooking, colouring, programming or crafts.
- If you get something wrong, forgive yourself. You can try again.
- Accept compliments by saying 'thanks!' instead of disagreeing.

- Smile at yourself in the mirror and tell yourself you are OK – even if it's hard to do or feels weird!
- If you catch yourself thinking negative thoughts, try reversing them. Change, 'I'm useless,' to, 'Actually, I am quite good at running/thinking up stories/baking', or whatever you do best.

I really like my haircut.

I enjoy cooking – I'm going to do it more often.

Mental health and illness

Mental health is the health of your mind, thoughts, emotions and behaviour. Normally, these things work well. But if you have a mental illness, they can become painful, confusing or out of control.

Mental illnesses

There are many types of mental ill health, ranging from mild problems like short-term stress, to more serious ones like depression. Here are some of them:

Bipolar disorder
Switching between depression and an excitable or 'manic' state.

Stress
Feeling pressured or overwhelmed, which can make you irritable and emotional.

Depression
Feeling low, numb, empty, or that you have no feelings at all.

Eating disorder
Obsessing about food, and sometimes eating too much or too little.

Anxiety
Out-of-control worrying or panic.

Schizophrenia
A severe illness that affects how a person thinks, feels and acts. It can cause confusion and hallucinations (seeing or hearing things that are not really there).

OCD
(obsessive-compulsive disorder)
A very strong urge to repeat obsessive thoughts or behaviours, such as hand-washing.

At least a quarter of people will have a mental health problem during their lifetime. Most people recover, or learn to live with the problem.

It's normal!

Though mental illness has not always been talked about much, it's actually very common. Almost everyone gets stressed or anxious sometimes – and most people have difficult times in their lives. However, people often hide their true feelings and don't talk about them. This means that when someone has a mental health problem, it can seem as if they are the only one experiencing it.

What causes mental illness?

Mental illness can have many different causes. Often, it's caused by a number of things happening together. They can include...

- Traumatic events, such as the death of someone close or family breakdown
- Feeling trapped or out of control
- Being abused or treated badly
- Trying to do too much – sometimes called 'burnout'
- Experiencing low self-esteem (see pages 8–9)
- Not having the right balance of chemicals in your brain
- Coming from a family where mental illness is common
- Taking certain drugs or becoming an addict, which can cause mental illness.

Staying mentally healthy

There are lots of ways to look after your mental health and help yourself to avoid illness. Many of them are simple things you can do every day.

- Get plenty of exercise
- Get enough sleep
- Eat healthily and regularly
- Remember to relax and breathe deeply
- Spend time with friends and spend time doing things you enjoy
- 'Switch off' from worries and tasks by reading, watching TV or playing a game
- Talk to someone about any worries or problems you have.

Are you crazy?

Mental illness is also called madness. Some people laugh at others for being 'mad', 'crazy' or 'nuts', or use these words as insults. This stigma, or disapproval, means people are sometimes scared to talk about mental health problems. But this is changing. There is now much more understanding of mental illness and how common it is. If you are worried about your mental health, it's a good idea to see a doctor, as there is often a lot they can do to help.

Stress

We all talk about stress in our daily lives. You will have heard people saying, 'Aaarggh, I'm so stressed about the exam!' or, 'Stop singing. You're stressing me out!' or, 'Mr Walker is such a stress-head.' But what is stress, exactly?

Good and bad

Stress isn't always a bad thing. It's actually a natural response to dangerous or difficult situations, and it exists to help us survive.

For example, if you're in an earthquake, the danger and panic makes you extremely stressed. Your body releases chemicals that make your heart beat faster to give you a burst of energy, which will help you run to safety faster than you normally could.

Phew! Made it!

However, lots of other things can make us feel stressed too. Things like worrying about friendships or schoolwork, or arguing with a sibling or parent, can also release those stress chemicals. They can build up and lead to a panicky, wound-up feeling that won't go away.

What it feels like

Stress affects different people in different ways, but the most common signs and symptoms are:

- Feeling breathless, with a tight chest
- Feeling panicky, or unable to stop worrying
- Feeling moody, irritable or snappy
- Trouble concentrating
- Trouble sleeping
- Bad dreams, or repetitive dreams about your worries

- Obsessing over decisions or problems
- Bursting into tears over something small
- Losing your appetite, or wanting to comfort-eat
- Nibbling your nails or skin, or pulling hairs out of your head.

Stress and your body

When stress chemicals build up in your body, they can be bad for your physical health as well as your mental health. Stress can cause headaches and stomach aches. It can also weaken your immune system, so you are more likely to catch bugs and feel run-down.

Teenage stress

When you're a teenager, there can be a lot of stressful things going on in your life. You might worry and stress about exams, choosing school subjects, what will happen in the future, friendships and relationships, and your changing body. With hormones, brain changes and mood swings to deal with too, it's no wonder teenagers often feel stressed out!

The stress scales

You need some stress in your life, to motivate you and get you moving. But to stop it getting too much, you have to balance it out with relaxation, which calms you down. It can help to think of a set of scales. On one side are all the things that stress you out. To balance them out, you have to add relaxing, calming and fun things onto the other side. Check out these scales to see what kinds of things might work best for you.

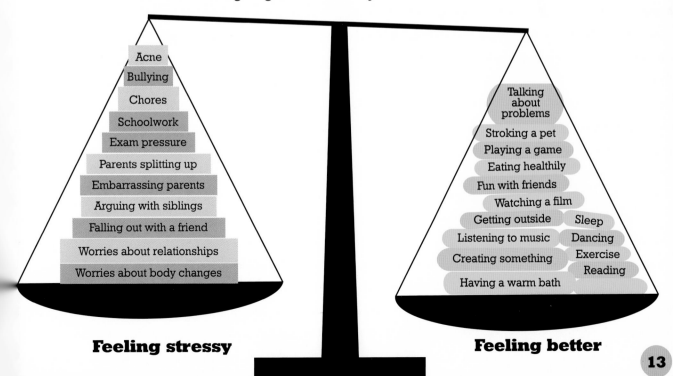

Acne
Bullying
Chores
Schoolwork
Exam pressure
Parents splitting up
Embarrassing parents
Arguing with siblings
Falling out with a friend
Worries about relationships
Worries about body changes

Talking about problems
Stroking a pet
Playing a game
Eating healthily
Fun with friends
Watching a film
Getting outside   Sleep
Listening to music   Dancing
Creating something   Exercise
                      Reading
Having a warm bath

Feeling stressy

Feeling better

Depression

People sometimes use the world 'depressed' to mean a bit sad, grumpy or disappointed. But that's very different from true depression. It's a serious mental illness that can go on for a long time, and it can have a big impact on daily life.

Down low

Depression literally means feeling 'pushed down' – having a very low, sad mood that won't go away. Sometimes, it can make people feel numb and empty instead, as if they have no emotions at all.

What's it like?

The signs and symptoms of depression can include:

Loss of appetite, or eating a lot

Feeling like there's no point in doing anything

Trouble concentrating

Feeling totally exhausted, with no energy

Sleeplessness

Feeling sad and despairing

Feeling numb or empty

Feeling irritable, angry or guilty

The impact of depression

Depression, especially if it's severe, can really affect the life of the sufferer, and those around them. It can make people –

• Avoid parties or other social occasions and stop going out
• Miss appointments
• Stop taking care of themselves
• Neglect schoolwork
• Upset others by seeming grumpy or selfish – although this is not the sufferer's fault
• Not want to do anything at all, or even get out of bed.

Why does it happen?

Like other metal illnesses, depression can be caused by many different things. Upsetting life events, abuse, bullying, low self-esteem and stress can all play a part. Sometimes, depression happens by itself, for no obvious reason. It can run in families too.

Self-harm

People with depression sometimes cut or hurt themselves – although self-harming does not necessarily mean that you are depressed. It can be a way that some people try to cope with difficult feelings or situations.

However, self-harming is, of course, not very good for you. It can cause dangerous injuries or infections, and leave scars. It may sometimes release stored up emotions, but is often followed by even worse feelings about yourself.

For anyone who has started self-harming, talking to a trusted friend, teacher or doctor is a good idea.

Suicide

Suicide is when someone deliberately ends their own life. It's a very drastic thing to do, and is very upsetting for other people. It can happen if someone is very depressed and has lost hope, and can see no other way to end their unhappiness.

If someone talks about ending their life, or becomes obsessed with death, it may mean they are planning suicide. It's important to tell a trusted adult about it and try to get help for the person.

Most people get better from severe depression. Although they might feel there is no hope at the time, they will probably look back and be glad they got through it.

Getting help

There are two main treatments for depression. They are often used together.

Medicine
Medicines called anti-depressants work by rebalancing the chemicals in the brain.

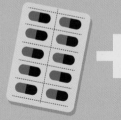

Therapy
This means talking to a doctor or counsellor. They can help the sufferer come to terms with whatever has made them depressed, and learn to manage their feelings.

Anxiety

Anxiety means worrying, feeling nervous and feeling scared. It's one of the most common mental health problems of all.

Worrying

Of course, everyone worries sometimes – that's normal. It can even be useful. If you weren't worried about accidents, you wouldn't cross the road carefully, for example.

However, worrying can become a problem if it gets out of control. It can start to affect what you do, and stop you from enjoying life. Some people worry so much that they find it difficult to leave their home.

What are you worried about?

If you suffer from anxiety, you might worry about all kinds of things. Teenagers often worry about things like...

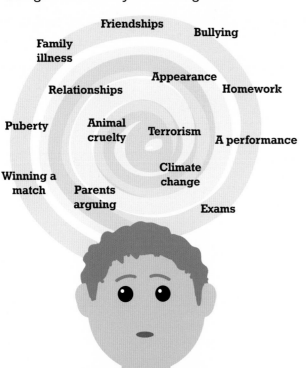

Friendships
Bullying
Family illness
Appearance
Relationships
Homework
Puberty
Animal cruelty
Terrorism
A performance
Winning a match
Climate change
Parents arguing
Exams

Some people also worry a lot about things that are very unlikely to happen, like getting a rare disease or a meteorite landing on them.

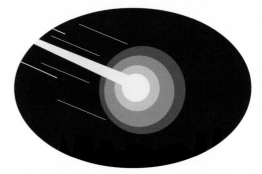

These are 'irrational' worries – they're so unlikely, spending a lot of time worrying about them doesn't make much sense. But if you have severe anxiety, worries like these can feel just as real and upsetting as any other.

Anxiety problems

Anxiety can also come in some other forms, or lead to other problems.

Phobias

A phobia is an extreme, irrational fear of something. It could be anything – open spaces, spiders, being sick or even baked beans!

OCD, or obsessive-compulsive disorder

The sufferer may feel they can control their worries by obsessively going through repeated actions, checks or routines.

I need to wash my hands four times.

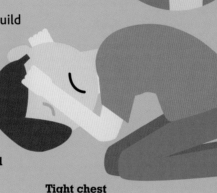

Panic attacks

Anxiety can make stress chemicals build up in your body until you feel overwhelmed by sudden panic. Panic attacks are harmless, but they can feel really scary.

A panic attack can include...

Tense muscles

Sense of dread

Pounding heart and fast breathing

Tight chest

What can you do?

Like depression, anxiety can sometimes be treated with medicines, or with therapy where you talk about your feelings.

A treatment called CBT (cognitive behavioural therapy) teaches you to learn to spot when you are worrying, and distract or redirect your thoughts.

A form of meditation called mindfulness (see pages 22–23) can also help. It involves pausing to think about and accept the feelings you are experiencing, then letting them go.

Taking good care of yourself can help with anxiety. Exercise and fresh air, eating well, and allowing plenty of time for sleep are especially useful.

If you feel anxious a lot of the time, a doctor may be able to help.

Food and fitness

Two of the best things you can do to stay mentally healthy are to eat a wide range of foods, and do some exercise.
But how do these things help your mind?

Your mind may sometimes feel like a separate thing, but it's closely linked to your body. Food and exercise help your brain and mind in lots of different ways.

Exercise

Exercise makes your body release chemicals called endorphins that make you feel happy.
It has many stress-busting effects too...

It increases blood flow to your brain, helping it to work better.

It makes your body tired, so you sleep better, which reduces stress.

Achieving exercise goals can help with self-esteem.

Being in a sports team helps you feel connected to others.

Playing a game, running, swimming or dancing can give you a break from whatever's on your mind.

Spending time outdoors, whether you are walking at a slow pace or running at speed, improves wellbeing.

Food

Hunger can make you stressed and jittery, but eating properly helps you stay calm. Cooking and eating with family or friends can be fun and relaxing. Eating a wide range of food helps your brain and body get all the nutrients they need.

Healthy fats help your brain to work well and are found in foods including olive oil, avocados and nuts.

Fruit and vegetables contain vitamins and minerals that can help your mood.

Calcium, found in dairy foods such as cheese, milk and yoghurt, also helps your brain to work well.

Magnesium helps you feel less anxious. It is found in foods including bananas and dark chocolate.

Carbohydrates, for example bread, rice, potatoes and pasta, give you energy to get things done.

Zinc can reduce depression and is found in foods including seafood and pulses.

Eating and exercise disorders

Mental health problems can sometimes arise around eating and exercise. Like other mental illnesses, they are not the sufferer's fault.

Anorexia nervosa (often called anorexia)
This illness makes people want to avoid eating. They often lose a lot of weight.

Binge eating disorder or BED
Sufferers feel compelled to binge-eat, or eat far too much at once.

Bulimia nervosa (often called bulimia)
Someone with bulimia may binge, then deliberately vomit or avoid eating for a while.

Exercise addiction
The desire to constantly improve can tip over into exercise addiction. Sufferers feel compelled to exercise all the time, and feel guilty if they don't.

Feelings like these can be hard to talk about. But like other mental health problems, they can be treated, and people do get better. If you think you or someone you know might have a problem like this, talking to a doctor, parent or teacher you trust is a good idea.

Assertiveness

'Assertiveness' means saying what you mean, and asking for what you want, in a simple, straightforward way.

Ways of talking

It might sound obvious, but the fact is, people often communicate and behave in ways that are not very assertive. Instead, they get angry. Or they stay quiet because they don't want to cause a fuss or an argument. Or they pretend to agree, but secretly feel annoyed.

Does any of this sound familiar? We all do these things sometimes. But they can cause problems. If you bottle up what you really think, you can end up feeling ignored and unimportant. If you get angry, stress chemicals will build up.

Self-esteem

How we talk to other people is closely linked to our self-esteem (see page 8). If you don't feel as if you matter, it's hard to believe people will listen to you. If you think people don't like you, it's easy to take things personally, and get cross.

Learning to be more assertive – to express yourself clearly and calmly – is good for your self-esteem. It helps you to avoid stress and upset, and encourages people to treat you fairly. You'll also find it helps other people take you more seriously, and listen to you more.

I think I need a bit of help with this assignment.

Not being assertive

Here are some examples of how people can behave when they're NOT being assertive.

Aggressive, or angry

This coffee is rubbish! I'm never coming HERE again!

How does it make you feel?
Worked up, agitated, stressed.

Manipulative, or sneaky

I didn't want to go on this walk. If I walk slowly they might leave me at home next time.

How does it make you feel?
Lonely, annoyed, resentful.

Passive, or giving in

I told them I hate mushrooms – but I suppose I have to eat them now. Hmph.

How does it make you feel?
Defeated, sad, unimportant.

Try it!

Being assertive sounds simple, but it can be hard to do. Here are a few tips, and some examples that you could practise saying out loud.

I know you want me to come on the walk but I'm saying no today.

- Say what you mean, simply and straightforwardly.
- Talk honestly about how you feel about things.
- If you mean no, it's OK to say no.
- There's no need to apologise or make excuses for what you have to say.
- Be polite and kind, but firm.
- Suggest sensible solutions or compromises.

Learning to talk to people in an assertive way takes practice, but will help build confidence and self-esteem.

Excuse me. This coffee tastes funny. Please could I have a new one?

I don't like mushrooms, so I'll leave them, but the rest looks lovely.

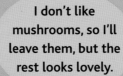

Mindfulness

Meditating means a kind of calm, focused thinking that can help you relax and de-stress. Mindfulness is a type of meditation that's often used today.

Being mindful

The word 'mindful' means aware or thoughtful. The idea of mindfulness is to be aware of what you are feeling and experiencing, and accept it, without judgment. Whatever sensations, thoughts and feelings you are having, you try to just accept them, and let them go.

I'm feeling a bit tired.

I'm glad it's the holidays!

My feet are chilly.

I'm still annoyed with Kai.

How does that help?

Many people find mindfulness helps them deal with things like stress, anxiety, panic and low self-esteem.

These things can make feelings build up and get on top of you. It's as if they won't stop bothering you. You might try to shut them out or push them away – but it doesn't work.

With mindfulness, you don't try to push feelings away, or label them as 'bad'. By simply accepting them, they become less frightening. Then you let them go, and make space for other feelings.

I can't sleep! I can't stop stressing about next week!

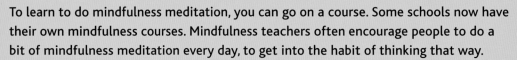

Mindfulness meditation

To learn to do mindfulness meditation, you can go on a course. Some schools now have their own mindfulness courses. Mindfulness teachers often encourage people to do a bit of mindfulness meditation every day, to get into the habit of thinking that way.

Try it!

This simple exercise will let you try a bit
of mindfulness for yourself.

Sit somewhere comfortable. Relax and breathe deeply.
Think about your body and senses. What can you see, hear,
smell, taste or touch? What emotions are you feeling?

Imagine you're a mountain, and your experiences are
like the weather. Thoughts, sensations and feelings
blow past, like the wind and the rain. They touch
you and you feel them. Then, they pass by.

> Remember,
> all feelings are OK. Even if
> you're feeling embarrassed,
> annoyed or bored!
> They're just feelings.

Using mindfulness

You can also use mindfulness in everyday life. For example, when you feel stressed and overwhelmed,
try pausing, taking a deep breath, and asking yourself, 'What am I really feeling, right now?'

This can help you 'reset' your mind and avoid getting stressed or worked up.
It can also help you understand your feelings, and explain them to others
calmly – turning tense moments into more positive ones.

> Don't worry if
> you find mindfulness
> difficult. It isn't always
> easy to do at first.

> Come on love,
> we'll be late for
> your concert!

> Arrrggh I'm
> COMING!
> You're always
> nagging!

> Hang on...
> what am I really
> feeling? My stomach
> is jittery... I feel a bit
> sick. I'm so nervous.

> Sorry for
> shouting Mum...
> I'm just really
> nervous.

> Oh sweetheart, it's
> OK. You'll be great.

Talking about it

There are lots of ways to look after your mental health, and to treat mental illnesses. One of the most important of all is one of the simplest – to talk about how you are feeling.

Not wanting to talk

However, although it's simple, people often find talking about their mental health isn't easy. Why is that? There are several reasons.

'Snap out of it!'

Mental health problems can change behaviour, for example by making people feel angry, avoid eating, or even harm themselves. We're brought up to feel we should control our own behaviour. So sufferers can feel guilty or ashamed, and that they should be able to just stop it, or 'snap out of it'.

'Crazy person'

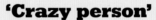

On top of that, there's the stigma attached to mental illness. People might be afraid they'll be laughed at, or that others will think they are pathetic, crazy or scary.

'No one cares'

And, if you have low self-esteem and feel worthless, it can be hard to believe anyone will understand, or be able to help.

'Big boys don't cry'

Experts say it can be especially hard for boys, as they are often brought up to think they shouldn't talk about feelings, cry, or appear weak.

Because of all of this, people who are having a hard time with their thoughts and feelings often don't tell anyone. They may bottle the feelings up inside, and try to cope alone.

Unfortunately, this can make mental and emotional problems worse.

Opening up

Being able to let the feelings out, tell someone about them, and have them understand, can be a huge relief.

- It makes the sufferer feel cared about.
- Sharing thoughts and feelings can make them less overwhelming.
- It lets the person you're talking to know what's wrong, so they can look after you.
- It can be the first step to getting medical help, if it's needed.

People to talk to

If you want to talk about a mental health problem, the first step is to choose someone kind and trustworthy.

Teachers or coaches
You might not like all your teachers, but if you have a kind, sympathetic one, they can be a great support.

Friends and siblings
Friends, siblings, or a boyfriend or girlfriend can be very supportive, especially if you want to moan about your parents!

Relatives
Sometimes an aunt or grandparent might understand you better than your parents do.

Doctors and health professionals
Doctors understand mental health problems, and know how to help.

Parents
If you have a close, caring parent, they are a really good person to talk to.

Helplines
If you feel there's no one you can talk to, there are helplines you can phone and websites where you can get support. You can find some of them on page 31 of this book.

If someone comes to you and explains that they are feeling stressed, anxious or depressed, you can help by staying calm, listening to them and asking about their feelings. You may not be able to solve all their problems, but having a friend to talk to can be a big help.

Healthy and happy for life

More and more, mental health is being seen the way it should be – as just a normal part of our general health.

Body and mind

The health of your mind, thoughts and emotions is important – just as important as the health of your body.

And just like physical health, you can look after it, talk about it, and get help with any problems that might come up.

Mental health for life

When you're a teenager, life can be very stressful at times. Some of the advice and tips in this book may be especially helpful as you grow up.

However, caring about your mental health isn't just for teenagers. It's important to look after it throughout your life. In the future, you may face difficult situations that can affect the way you feel.

If a relationship breaks up, or you lose someone you love, it can lead to low self-esteem, depression or anxiety for a period of time.

Many jobs can be stressful too, especially if you have to work long or difficult hours.

Having a baby can be extremely stressful, and some people become depressed for a while afterwards. This is known as PND or post-natal depression.

Life events such as moving house, a job interview or unemployment can cause stress, worry or sleeplessness.

Taking care of yourself

The advice in this book is here to help you know what to do at those times, and how to keep yourself as calm and happy as possible from day to day.

• Developing assertiveness, mindfulness and good self-esteem will stand you in good stead for a mentally healthy life.

• Building in time for rest, relaxation and enjoyment will rebalance those stress scales, so that you can recover from the things that wear you out.

• Exercise, good food and good-quality sleep will always help to counteract stress and anxiety, and make you feel refreshed.

• Sharing your problems and talking them over with someone who cares will help to stop them getting you down.

Keep reading!

Of course, this is just a short book, and it can't cover every detail, or include all the mental health problems that exist. But there are plenty more books and websites out there that can. Some of these are listed on page 31.

Good luck... and look after yourself!

Support guide

Ways to stay mentally healthy

- Spend time outdoors
- Get plenty of exercise
- Get plenty of sleep
- Eat a wide range of different foods
- Eat regularly, and eat when you are hungry
- Keep your brain active – read, play games
- Be creative – make things, cook, draw, program, sew, write songs, poetry or stories

- Do things with friends
- Do group activities, like team sports, or being in a choir, drama group, orchestra or band
- Try to be honest with yourself about your feelings
- Talk to others about your feelings
- See a doctor if you are worried about your mental health

Ways to counteract stress, anxiety and worry

- Listen to music you love
- Read a gripping book that you can't put down
- Watch a funny film or TV show
- Stroke, cuddle or talk to a pet
- Have a drink of water, milk or tea
- Have a warm bubble bath
- Do something you are good at
- Go out in daylight or light indoor rooms brightly
- Look at yourself in the mirror, smile and say something kind to yourself

- Think of something you are happy about or grateful for
- Breathe slowly and deeply for a few minutes
- See friends and do something fun together
- Tell someone what you are worried or stressed about
- Dance and sing along to music
- Be mindful – stop and ask yourself how you are really feeling

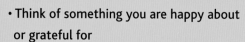

Getting help

There is a range of people you can talk to about mental health problems. They may be able to help, or support you to ask for more help.

- Friends
- Parents
- Siblings
- Relatives, such as a favourite auntie or grandparent
- Sports coaches or teachers
- A scout or guide leader or other club leader
- A teacher you like and trust at school

- A school counsellor
- A school medical or welfare officer
- A doctor or other healthcare worker
- A social worker
- A helpline (see page 31)

Helping a friend

If a friend turns to you for support with a mental health problem, it can be hard to know what to do. It will help them to share their feelings, but some mental illnesses are hard to treat and it could be stressful for you to try to look after the person all on your own.

- Encourage your friend to approach an adult about their problem as well.
- Talk to them about different ways to get support, such as those listed above.

- If you are really worried about a friend, it's OK to talk about it to a parent, teacher or other trusted adult yourself, to try to get them the help they need.

We're all different

People have different personalities and feelings, and things like stress, worry and low self-esteem can affect people in different ways. So there isn't a 'one size fits all' solution to mental health problems – it depends on the individual, and what works best for them. So, if you're trying to reduce stress, for example, try lots of different things, and see which you like best. You might find that exercise helps you the most – or writing, or baking, or a day out with a friend. By knowing yourself, and what you need, you can look after yourself and help yourself to stay healthy.

Glossary

abuse Cruel, violent or hurtful treatment.

anorexia nervosa (also called anorexia)
An eating disorder that makes people want to avoid eating.

antidepressants Medicines that work on the brain to treat depression or anxiety.

anxiety Severe or ongoing worry, panic or fear.

assertiveness Expressing yourself in a calm, confident way.

binge eating disorder (BED) An eating disorder that makes people want to overeat.

bipolar disorder A mental illness in which sufferers switch between depression and an excitable or 'manic' state.

bulimia nervosa (also called bulimia)
An eating disorder that makes people switch between eating too little, and eating too much, or eating too much and being sick.

burnout A state of stress and exhaustion caused by trying to do too much.

cognitive behavioural therapy (CBT)
A way of treating anxiety or other mental illnesses by recognising unwanted thoughts and using various techniques to distract yourself from them.

counsellor A person who is trained to listen to and help with personal and emotional problems.

depression A mental illness that causes ongoing feelings of sadness, numbness, exhaustion, despair or not wanting to take part in life.

eating disorder A type of mental illness that affects how and what people want to eat.

endorphins Chemicals released by the brain, often during exercise, which make you feel good.

hormones Chemicals your body releases to make some body parts work, grow or change.

immune system The body system that fights off germs and diseases.

meditation Thinking in a deliberate, calm, focused way to aid relaxation and reduce stress.

mental To do with the mind.

mental health The health of your mind and emotions.

mental illness Illness that affects your mind and emotions.

mindfulness Being aware of and accepting your feelings, as a way of reducing stress and anxiety.

obsessive-compulsive disorder (OCD)
A mental illness that makes sufferers want to repeat obsessive thoughts or behaviours, such as hand-washing.

panic attack An overwhelming feeling of panic, sometimes with a racing heartbeat, tense muscles, sweating, or feeling unable to breathe.

phobia An extreme irrational fear of something, such as spiders or bridges.

physical To do with the body.

plastic In relation to the brain, 'plastic' means able to change and be reshaped.

post-natal depression (PND) A form of depression that can affect women, and sometimes men, after having a baby.

schizophrenia A severe mental illness that can cause confusion and hallucinations.

self-esteem How you feel and what you believe about yourself.

self-harm Cutting yourself or hurting yourself in other ways, which can be a symptom of some mental illnesses.

stigma Disapproval from other people or society in general.

stress Mental or emotional tension or exhaustion.

suicide Ending one's own life deliberately.

 # Further information

Books

The Teenage Guide to Stress
by Nicola Morgan
Walker Books, 2014

Banish Your Self-Esteem Thief
by Kate Collins-Donnelly
Jessica Kingsley Publishers, 2014

Self-Esteem and Being YOU
by Anita Naik
Wayland, 2013

Mind Your Head
by Juno Dawson and Dr. Olivia Hewitt
Hot Key Books, 2016

Websites

Teenshealth: Mind
http://kidshealth.org/en/teens/your-mind/#cat20139

YoungMinds
http://www.youngminds.org.uk/

Teen Mental Health
http://teenmentalhealth.org/

YouthSpace Help and Advice
http://www.youthspace.me/help_and_advice

Note to parents and teachers:
Every effort has been made by the Publishers to ensure that these websites are suitable for children, that they are of the highest educational value, and that they contain no inappropriate or offensive material. However, because of the nature of the Internet, it is impossible to guarantee that the contents of these sites will not be altered. We strongly advise that Internet access is supervised by a responsible adult.

Helplines and support

Mind Infoline
http://www.mind.org.uk/information-support/helplines/
0300 123 3393

SANEline
http://www.sane.org.uk/#
0300 304 7000

Childline
http://www.childline.org.uk/Pages/Home.aspx
0800 1111

The Samaritans
http://www.samaritans.org/how-we-can-help-you/contact-us
116 123 (UK)
116 123 (Republic of Ireland)